NORMAN

Special Delivery

Karen Leahey

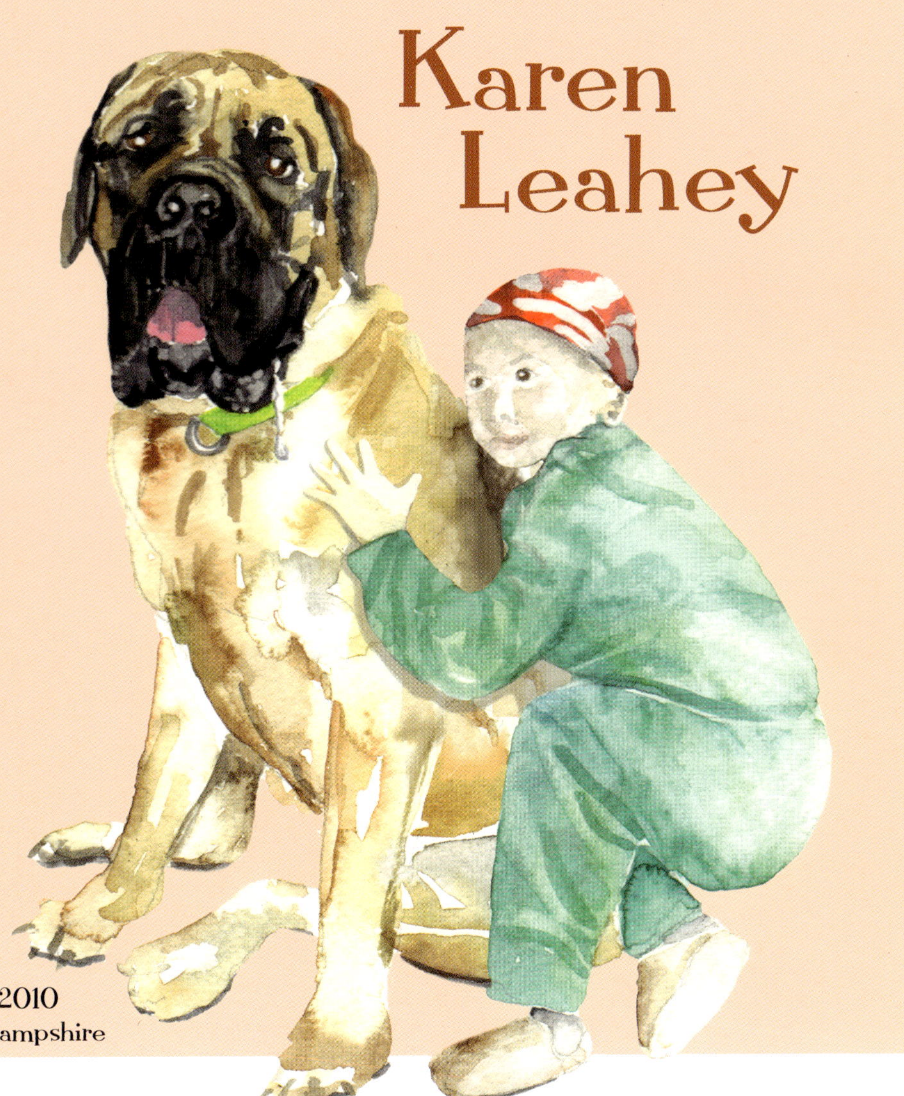

Peapod Press 2010
Exeter, New Hampshire

Peapod Press, an imprint of
PublishingWorks, Inc.,
151 Epping Road
Exeter, NH 03833

603-778-9883
www.publishingworks.com

Designed by: Birdy Graphics & Melodica Design

LCCN: 2010936243
ISBN-13: 978-0-9826911-7-5

Printed in the United States by Walsworth.

NORMAN

Special Delivery

Dedication:

Jada and Rachel

A Great Dane, and a Terrific Human respectively.

The stork popped a cork.
Yup, that was the only explanation the nurses and I could come up with when we discovered the wee pup in our hospital's nursery.

Whatever the reason, he was as cute as a button, so we kept him.

I named him Norman.

I took care of the little guy, with help from the rest of the staff.

Nurse Betty made up a bed and bought a stuffed toy for him.

The night shift set out his breakfast every morning.

The doctors
made sure
he stayed
healthy
and strong.

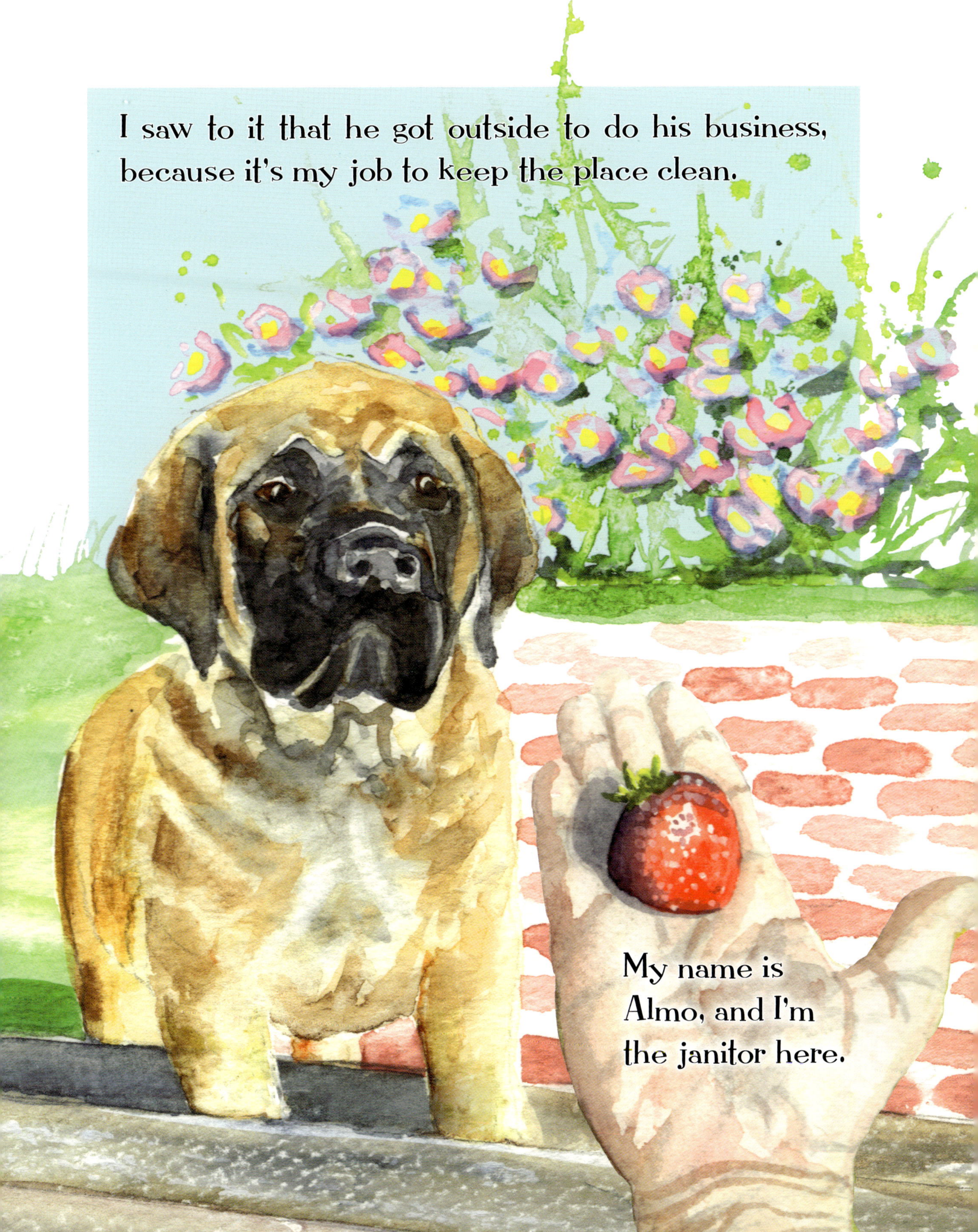
I saw to it that he got outside to do his business, because it's my job to keep the place clean.
My name is Almo, and I'm the janitor here.

When he was a pup, I took him along on shopping trips.

He was my "little guy," but not for long.

He quickly outgrew that nickname.

Norman grew, and grew, and grew some more, until we wondered if he would ever stop.

Eventually, I just let him have the run of the hospital.

Going Up?

It was, after all, his home.

The security guards and staff pretended they didn't see Norman when he moseyed past them.

That was pretty ridiculous when you consider his awesome size.

Besides, hiding from people was not his specialty.

Of course, hospital visitors were startled to see the lion-sized creature, and shied away from him.

Some even asked me if he bit people.

"Nope," I answered."He swallows them whole."

Norman was not the only animal in the hospital.

There were all sorts of critters in our pet therapy program.

But Norman sure stood out.

Naturally, there is a size limit to be a therapy animal, but he came in just a hair under it.

Therapy pets must fit through the door.

One day, Norman met Buddy, a service dog.

Buddy explained that any animal could do pet therapy.

But he had to behave himself!

"You can't be running up and down the halls," warned Buddy.

This would not be a problem for Norman, because he preferred taking naps anyway.

Buddy further explained what the rules were,

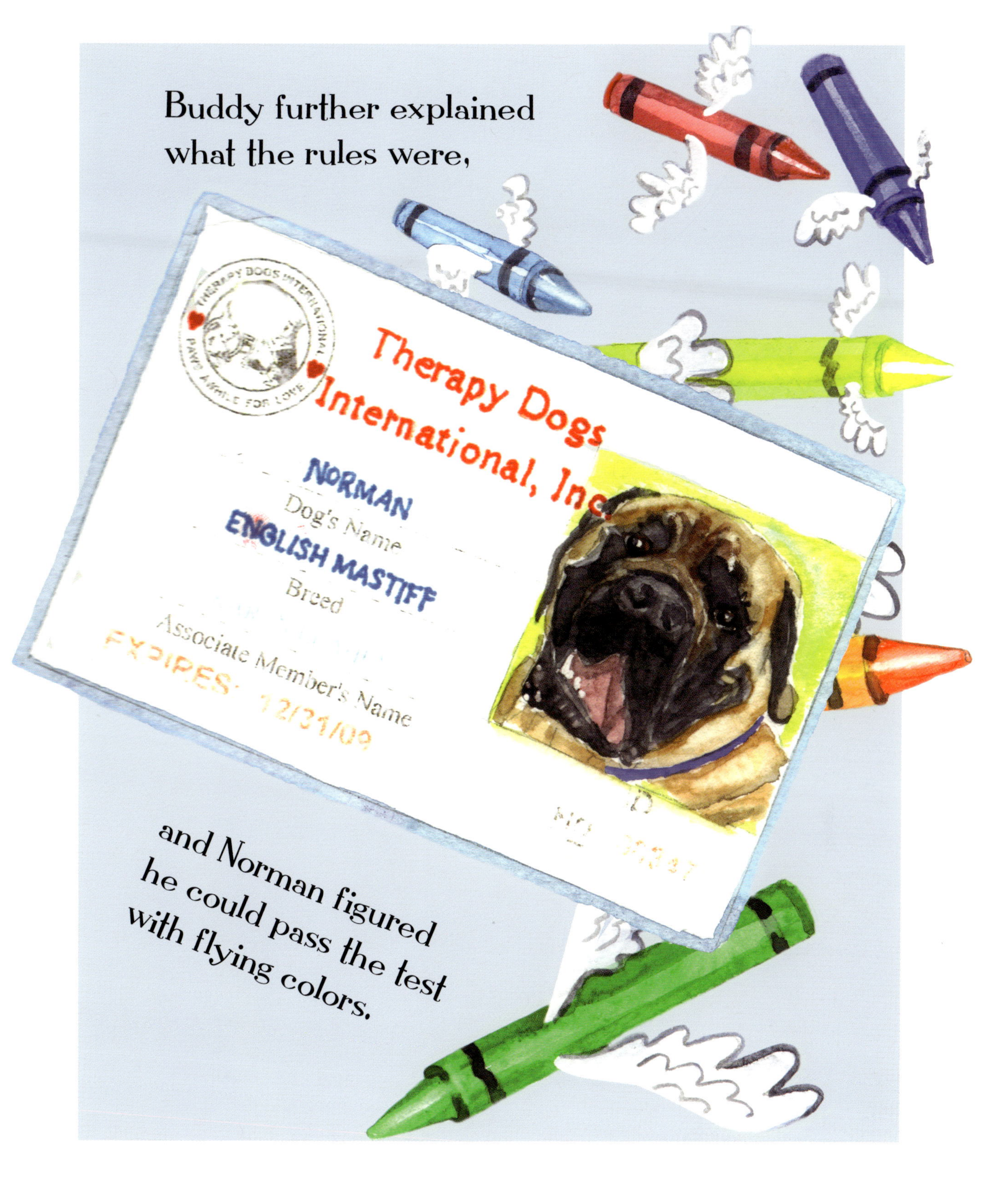

and Norman figured he could pass the test with flying colors.

He then took it upon himself to start visiting and entertaining patients during their stay in the hospital. I know this, because I followed him...

or rather I followed his drool, which of course I promptly mopped up.

My work was cut out for me
when we passed the cafeteria.

Our patients were not in the least bit frightened by the big dog.

They all recognized him for what he was on the inside: a gentle giant with a big heart.

To top it off, he was a real crowd pleaser.

I overheard Mr. Brown speak at great length with Norman about his aches and pains, and felt all the better for it.

Norman listened patiently.

Johnny was scared of the tests a doctor wanted to perform,

but relaxed after Norm played "leap dog" with him.

There were occasional mishaps, like when Norman couldn't maneuver between the tight-fitting beds. Eventually, he got the hang of it.

Ms. Jones shared her meatball sandwich with Norman, and showed off pictures of her grandchildren.

Norman agreed that they were indeed adorable because, after all,

there was still dessert.

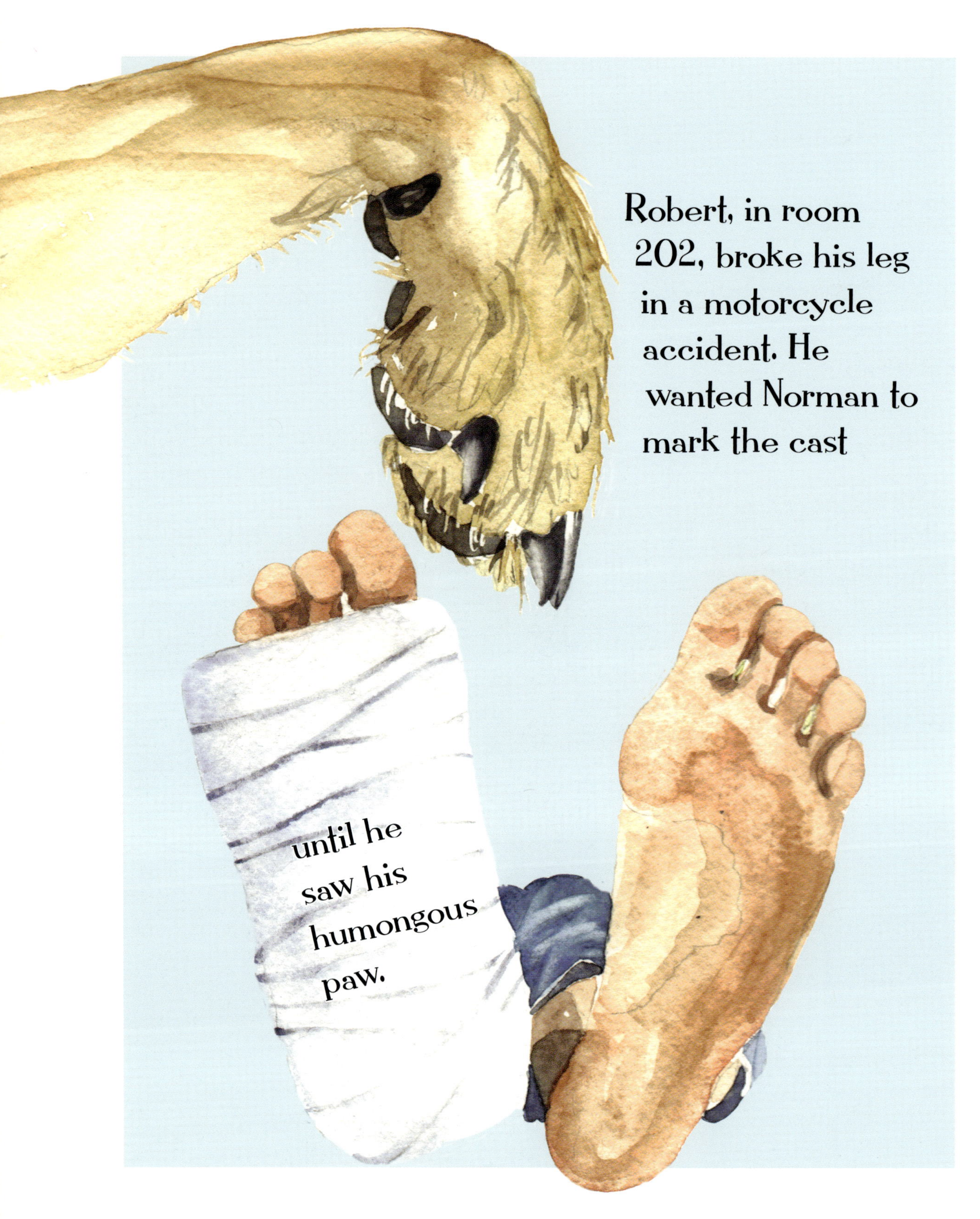

Robert, in room 202, broke his leg in a motorcycle accident. He wanted Norman to mark the cast until he saw his humongous paw.

After helping Old Man Bill back into bed, Norman tucked the covers around him ever so gently.

Bill was very appreciative.

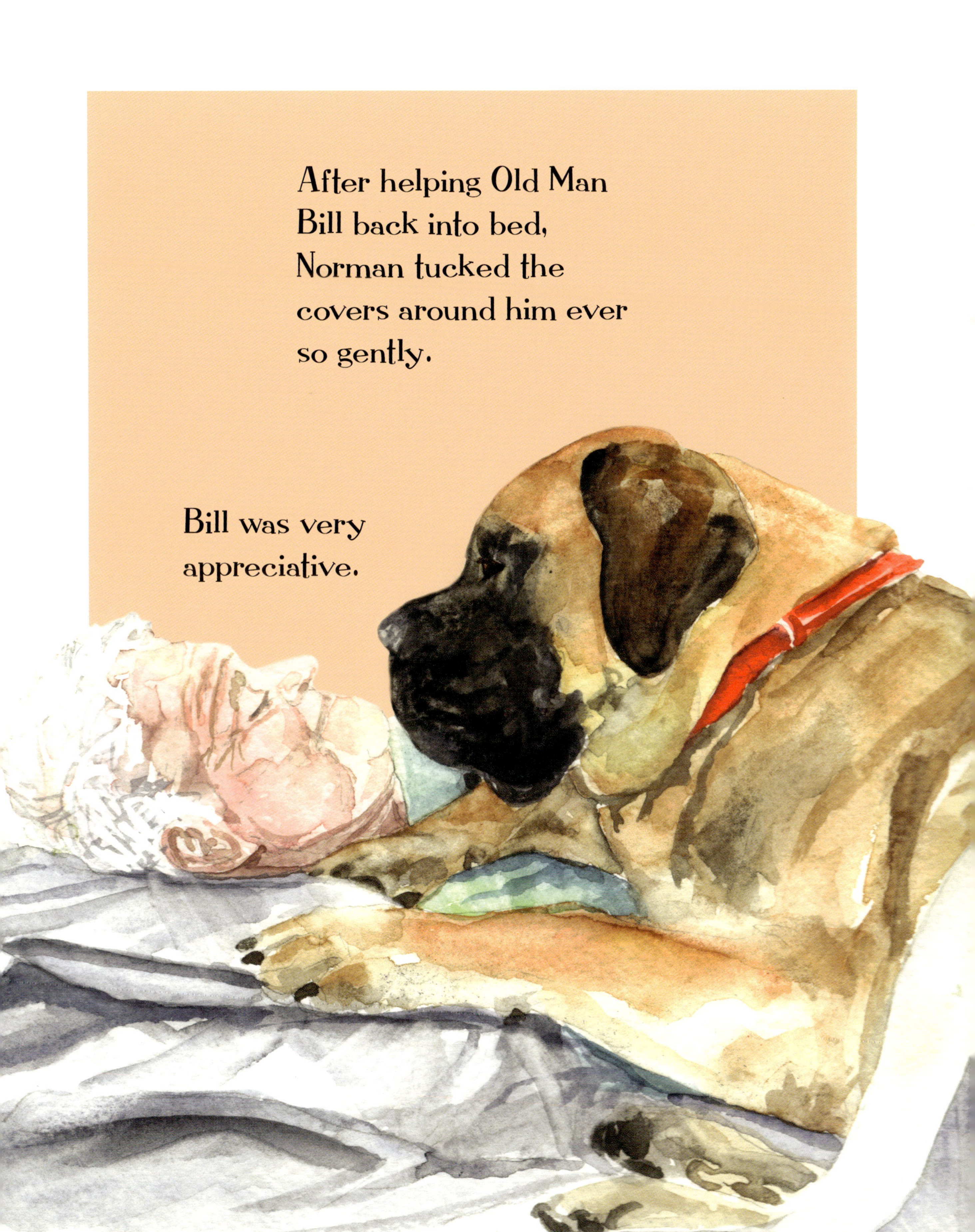

As was Rachel, when she discovered a new best friend to tell her innermost secrets to.

He played cards with young Frank,

until he spied the bag of goodies a visitor had left behind.

Norman loved marsh-mallows, and borrowed some to share with the rest of the kids.

Of course, he would not be returning them.

He read to Suzy,

until she dozed...

...then promptly fell asleep in the bed next to her.

Justin laughed at
Norm's silly jokes
until there were
tears in his eyes.

ALL of the children, even the smallest and youngest,

understood that
the gentle
giant
wouldn't
hurt a
fly.

Norman now spends his days walking the halls with patients,

or simply

keeping them company when they are lonely.

If they're real lucky, he might even plant a big wet kiss on them. He does that very well.

So, puppies come into this world with a plan and a purpose. Some brighten our days, and some take care of us.

Apparently, the stork didn't pop a cork. He knew exactly what he was doing when he dropped "the little guy" off at our hospital.

Who will he drop off next?

About the Author

Karen Leahey, a self-taught artist, lives with Norman and husband Bill in New Jersey. She first met Norman when he was just ten weeks old and weighed a mere thirty-two pounds. It was love at first sight. She drives him to various medical facilities for his volunteer work, with the Medical Center being their favorite.

www.normansbooks.com

About Norman

Norman was born January 20, 2007. He is a volunteer at Monmouth Medical Center in Long Branch, New Jersey. His goal in life is to beat the long distance slobber flinging world record. Other than that, his favorite things to do are eat, nap, and hang out with the local deer. He lives in Monmouth County, New Jersey, with his people, Karen and Bill Leahey.